THE LC SCAPEGOAT

Stations of the Cross for Today

CHRISTOPHER IRVEN

Brimstone Press

First published in 2007
by Brimstone Press
PO Box 114
Shaftesbury SP7 8XN

www.brimstonepress.co.uk

Designed by Linda Reed and Associates
Shaftesbury, Dorset, SP7 8NE
Tel: 01747 850487
Email: lindareedassoc@btconnect.com

Printed by J H Haynes and Co Ltd
Sparkford, Somerset, BA22 7JJ
Tel: 01963 440635
Email: bookproduction@haynes.co.uk

ISBN 978-1-906385-02-6

All images in this book, copyright
exemptions and the necessary permissions
from Private Collections, were obtained
and supplied by
The Bridgeman Art Library
17–19 Garway Road
London W2 4PH

Contents

Acknowledgements

Several years ago I was asked to lead some Confirmation candidates through the Stations of the Cross in a school chapel. It was the last event in a weekend retreat programme packed with interest and activity, on what promised to be a hot summer's afternoon at the local school. They would be tired and looking forward to the final tea-break before going home, and the last thing these young and enthusiastic adults needed was me simply droning through one of the CTS pamphlets available for the purpose – a soggy end to a lively retreat. Some serious preparation was called for, a 'Stations' that truly spoke to young people in a language they could understand. From their reaction, and those of the other adults leading them that weekend, the effort paid off. And because I or other catechists might be involved in similar programmes in the future, I tidied up my notes into a first draft. That draft would eventually become this book.

That was more than ten years ago. Since then the draft has been altered often, in a process involving many people – friends, family, acquaintances who have kindly offered advice and encouragement. Particularly I should mention my friend Pierrette Plumridge with whom I have exchanged many ideas. I have also been strongly influenced by the clarity and insights of Dom Sebastian Moore of Downside. Not only has he brought me to understand ideas I would probably not have dreamt of, but he has also introduced me to the writings of René Girard who might yet be acclaimed a Doctor of the Church and whose understanding of 'what was going on' at our Redemption has been nothing short of revelatory. Most of all, perhaps, I am grateful to those who have encouraged me to press on with publication, among whom were Father Peter Gallagher SJ of Heythrop College, and the late Cardinal Basil Hume.

The author and publisher wish to thank St Pauls Publishing for permission to copy Father John Jacob Raub's prayer from his book *Who told you that you were naked?* as the prayer before the Stations. The author also acknowledges the inspiration for two of the meditations (Stations 8 and 9) that he received from reading *The Golgotha of Jasna Gora in the Third Millennium* by J.D. Gracz.

Christopher N.L. Irven

Introduction

For centuries, meditation on the Passion of Christ has been a luxury for the pious. Abbot Chapman, one of our greatest modern teachers of contemplative prayer, sounded another note when he asked: which is the greater love, to enjoy meditating on the Passion or saying 'I can't bear to think about it'? Now we are beginning to see the crucified figure as the universal scapegoat who pays for the way we live and organise the world, destructively of our mother earth, as we are now coming to realise. Chris Irven's meditations are a wonderful exercise in bringing the praying mind into this new focus. Some of the artworks he uses do this in a stunning way, especially the painting of the stripping of Jesus which puts out disturbing feelers into the unconscious and evokes memories of the playground. A name which I hope is becoming a household word for the follower of Jesus is that of René Girard, who brought about a Copernican Revolution in anthropology by pointing to the scapegoat-victim, ingrained in our thinking, as the solution to our problems, especially in this age of terrorism. The disciple of Jesus is invited, as the Spirit will guide him or her, to make their personal identification of Jesus with their implicit scapegoat – implicit, for it doesn't have to be any particular person – and so, in finally recognizing him, to be rid of the sickness for good and all. But – and this is vital – the purpose of this exercise is not to induce guilt but to allow you to became a disciple all the way past Golgotha to life eternal, allowing your ego's Jesus, the Loving Scapegoat, to die in you and have him risen to be your life. God has been our scapegoat, for us to crucify as St Paul says in his letter to the Romans: 'What we must realize is that our former selves have been crucified with him to destroy this sinful body and to free us from the slavery of sin.'

For me, meditation on the Passion is accompanied with 'The Power of Now' by Eckhart Tolle. Somehow – I don't quite know how – when I look at the Crucified with Easter eyes I am simultaneously looking at my 'ego's Jesus' as an inflatable toy, and I am pulling the stopper out to let him die and become life itself in me.

This may not suit you at all, it is only my way of doing what we disciples are called to do in this critical time: let go of the ego and enter into the fullness of his life in us. St Paul did this in a dramatic way. He saw everything he'd believed in, his whole pharisaic religion, summed up in Jesus its victim, and dying in Saul to rise in Paul as full and deathless life for others. And so he says to Timothy, 'If we have died with him, then we shall live with him.'

Here's another message of Paul's. 'Both Jew and pagan are justified… by being redeemed in Christ Jesus who was appointed by God to sacrifice his life to win reconciliation through faith.' Think deeply about that phrase I'm emphasising. Jesus is the scapegoat-victim of all humanity. How do I know this? By faith! By faith this universal victim becomes my victim. Faith, an act of total trust in God who knows what he's doing in me, enables me to 'take out' on Jesus (as the scapegoat of old took out the sins of Israel) all the violent feelings with which I react to the world – about tyranny wherever we turn throughout the planet. And faith, this act of total reliance on God, brings this Jesus, whom I am killing, alive in me in a wonderful new freedom we get first in dribs and drabs and then, with constant exercise, increasingly. That is what it means 'to win reconciliation through faith'.

To make the Stations is, gradually, to let God be crucified by you and brought to life in you.

Sebastian Moore

Foreword

There are many versions of the meditation called the fourteen Stations of the Cross (in fact some have fifteen, sixteen or even eighteen Stations), and that is not surprising. The challenge to human comprehension presented by this mystery of God's love is perhaps equalled only by that of the Eucharist, of which it is an inseparable part. It is therefore right that there should be many ways to try to come to terms with its meaning. But above all we should see the events of the suffering and death of Jesus, not as an historical episode depicted, say, in a moving film about someone we admire, but as a journey each of us has to make in company with our Lover, through our own life and death into the glory of the resurrection he won for us. In his letter to the Romans St Paul reminds us that we have been baptised into his death so that by dying with him we might be raised with him into glory. The Stations of the Cross should be about each of us on our life's pilgrimage, following as closely as we can in his footsteps. For that reason perhaps, this form of meditation should be used regularly as part of the practice of our faith and not just 'saved up' for Lent. Unless we recognize our Lord's crucifixion as something in which each of us is intimately involved, something in which we took (well, take) an active part, meditating on it will avail us little.

It's also for this reason that the form of the meditation we use should have an immediacy, an impact that speaks strongly to us. The form this impact takes will differ for each individual. For example my preference in prayer is for an idiom that's modern rather than Victorian poetic, which is why I have called this book 'Stations of the Cross for Today'. Again, for the sake of immediacy we should not sanitise the crucifixion and the torture leading up to it in an attempt to ease our discomfort. Where I live, the Christian Churches enact the Passion of Jesus in the streets of the town on Good Friday. One of the things that carries great impact in this event is the cross, which is full scale and can just be lifted by a strong man. It is made of coarse timber stained with blood. The nails are long and crude, the hammer is heavy, the scourge a chilling implement of wood, leather and metal stained with blood, and the crown of thorns repels all but the most gingerly handling. These 'props' shock. People are arrested by them and they attract the curiosity of children and parents in a way ordinary theatrical costumes never could. They bring home the hideous reality of the manner in which Jesus died. They make it immediate. For the thoughtful there is a nagging feeling we were involved… in murder.

Nevertheless, while it's important to try to appreciate the intensity of Christ's suffering we should not allow our minds to be so swamped by it that we forget the lessons to be learnt. The theology matters: it would be a pity to lose it in a surfeit of pious language and hand wringing. His submission to passion and death was the willing act of Christ who was human as well as divine. Through his resurrection it will transform the human nature of which he is head, *the* Adam. It will force us to face up to the interdependence, as old as mankind itself, of victim and persecutor that we call the scapegoat syndrome; and by acknowledging it ultimately end it. Something as wonderful and redeeming as that should never be forgotten in our just and necessary compassion for our Saviour.

Again, we can use the Stations to reflect on the wonderful mystery of his pierced side. Jesus said, 'Unless a grain of wheat falls to the ground and dies, it remains only a single grain; but if it dies, it yields a rich harvest' (Jn 12:24). From his lanced heart – his dying – flow out blood and water, the birth-flush of his Church. The water from his side is our baptism. These and so many other mysteries of his suffering and death are sources of great joy, and in our sorrow for the pain we cause him we should not deprive ourselves of these consolations.

Readers may question why some of the Stations are not more firmly based on scripture. Traditionally the Catholic Church has not done this. For example, the tradition of Veronica (anagram of *Vera Icon*, the True Image of our Saviour's face imprinted on her shawl) is not found in the Gospels. But then neither are the accounts of his several falls, or the meeting with his mother, the stripping and so on. But together with the Stations that have scriptural backing they provide us with episodes on which to base our thoughts and prayers. So we can make of them what we will and allow our imaginations to make us truly present on his journey.

I believe that Veronica, if she existed, would not have been permitted to remove the crown of thorns. This terrible mockery was composed of long, hard thorns far more lethal than our kindly North European ones, which is why I imagine the incident of her saving him from blinding. The bit about how he, his sight restored, recognized her whom he had once cured by his mud-and-spittle paste (borrowed from the Mark's and John's accounts of how he had cured a blind man) is pure whimsy. But it's an example of the way we might allow our private imaginings to wander in prayer and of how Jesus needs our compassion and help. He cured our blindness: We could have been Veronica; we would proudly have carried Simon's load.

As mentioned at the beginning, these thoughts are just one example of many of possible collections, some of which can be found in pamphlets at the back of our churches. They draw from some of these, from the gospels, and from my own thoughts informed by dozens of people throughout my life. The verses at the end of each station are taken from the *Stabat Mater* hymn traditionally sung in Catholic churches during this service. They have been included here, just another form of meditation on offer.

An act of sorrow

Dear Lord, you know how much I love you; but, more than that, how much you love me! Therefore, Jesus, do not let anything come between us. Forgive me my sins, and wash them away as if they had never been. Amen.

Prayer before the Stations

[from 'Who told you that you were naked?'
by Fr John Jacob Raub, OCSO].

Thank you, God, for becoming a human being –
     so I don't have to be like the gods.

Thank you for becoming finite, limited –
     so I don't have to be infinite, unlimited.

Thank you for becoming mortal –
     so I don't have to try to be immortal.

Thank you for becoming inferior –
     so I and others don't have to be superior.

For being weak –
     so I and others don't have to be strong.

For being imperfect –
     so I and others don't have to be perfect.

For being disapproved –
     so I and others don't have to be approved.

God, thank you for being wrong in people's eyes –
     so I and others don't have to be right.

For being a failure –
     so I and others don't have to succeed.

For being poor in every way –
     so I and others don't have to be rich in any way.

Christ on the Cross, thank you for being different from my idols, so I don't have to hate myself and others for being different from those images I have created to support me and hold me up.

Thank you for becoming all the things I think I should not be, so I don't have to kill myself and others trying to be all the things I think I should be.

Crucified God, thank you for becoming everything I despise about myself, so I can love myself and others in you.

I *can* love you – who by your humanity have joined yourself with me right at the point where I most dislike myself.

God – thank you for being crucified, so I can be free.

The Stations of the Cross

Ecce Homo (oil on canvas), by Antonio Ciseri (1821–91),
Galleria d'Arte Moderna, Florence

Pilate is in a quandary. He knows this exasperatingly silent man, whose kingly bearing and straight gaze make a mockery of the mocking inflicted on him by the soldiers, is completely innocent. His own rhetorical question about truth had been heartfelt despair, not confusion, but even that this Jesus let pass. His wife confides her misgivings to another woman in the right of the picture but knows her words will not carry enough weight to change his mind. Pilate pleads – yes, pleads – with the crowd to be reasonable. Fat chance! Since when was any mob reasonable, let alone this stiff-necked people? '*Look* at the man!' he shouts.

Jesus is condemned to death by me

What is happening here? Jesus had been dragged before the High Priest and the Pharisees who were determined to get even with him for exposing their hypocrisy. Now they had a chance to condemn him to death: he had claimed to be God, and blasphemy – which is how they saw it – meant death. But they hadn't the authority, so they had to get Pilate to do their dirty work for them. Pilate was a harassed politician whose main job was to keep the locals quiet and procure taxes for Rome. The Jews were always a bloody-minded lot, he reflected, and riots were a constant threat that had to be dealt with firmly. The last thing he needed before breakfast was a religious nut and a bunch of bickering priests, but what could he do? They knew how to use their authority to make life difficult for him and had already inflamed the crowd. Releasing Jesus could start a riot putting paid to his career. So… he washed his hands of it – literally – and condemned a man he knew to be innocent, brought before him out of spite by these lizards, to death on the city's rubbish dump. Sad, but expedient. Pax Romana is rough justice, or it's nothing.

Some politicians haven't changed much in 2000 years.

Great. So the death of Jesus was the fault of a cowardly and brutal (and pagan) Roman system, and spiteful Jewish leaders who ought to have known better. Which lets me off the hook.

But does it? This attitude of passing the buck won't do. It led to the hatred of Jews down the ages as the perfect scapegoats for our own uneasiness about what happened. And anyway, Jesus was a Jew. No, let's face it: *I* condemned Jesus to death. If I'd been the only miserable sinner on earth he'd have gone through the whole ghastly thing just for me. That is the terrible, uncompromising love I have to come to terms with in the face of my lukewarm and heartless response.

✚ ✚ ✚ ✚ ✚ ✚ ✚

Dear Jesus, I know human nature is shared as well as private. Responsibility for world events can never be completely attributed solely to others; and of all this world's events, that was never more true than of your crucifixion. Do not allow me to shut my eyes to my involvement in your death by blaming Pilate or the Jewish leaders at the time, let alone their nation then or now. For if I do, I deny that this stupendous act of your love was done for me.

Jesus, give us the honesty to face up to our personal complicity in your murder.

At the cross her station keeping,
stood the mournful mother weeping,
close to Jesus to the last.

Jesus embraces his cross

They give Jesus his cross. He is a man with a man's natural fear of death, and in particular the manner of dying. He sees in his mind's eye the nails being driven through his heels into the sides of the step at the foot of the cross so that the only way to take the weight off his arms to snatch a breath is to stand on this hideous hinge and gasp. He sees the cramps, and the slow and merciful suffocation that will eventually free him, and he shudders.

Yet he is God too. He sees this frightful gibbet that has held an empire in terrified submission for so long, a sign of human barbarity and fear and shame, transformed forever more into the greatest symbol of love and hope the world will ever know. He sees countless thousands of millions of people, the darling sheep of his pasture he loves more than his own life, saved by what he is about to do. He sees the blood and water that will flow out of his pierced heart like the blood and water in which a child is born, for from his death his Church will be born and in time will enfold all mankind throughout history into his heart. (But, above all from my perspective, he sees *me*.) It will all be worth it. He knows he can never turn back.

So what does he do? He takes the cross; he hugs it to himself; he *kisses* it. The soldiers think he's lost his marbles: the scourging can sometimes do that to a man. But I know better. After all, if the only way to save someone I dearly loved – such as my wife or children, mother or father, or a brother or sister in my family – was to die, wouldn't I accept it too? Of course. That's what love is all about, so what did I expect?

Jesus, Man-God, thanks to you and the Holy Spirit within us, we too are to be little men and women sharing your Divine Nature, little Man-Gods. So, like you we are entitled to have mixed feelings about the sufferings and hardships that come our way. Our happiness lies not in trying to avoid them for ultimately we cannot, but in accepting them willingly in loving imitation of you and then making the best of it. Help me not to make too much of a song and dance about my crosses or to be too indignant when I discover that my heaviest cross is myself.

Lord, give us the courage to be fully human, wholeheartedly embracing this nature which you have raised above the angels by making it your own.

> *Through her heart, his sorrow sharing,*
> *all his bitter anguish bearing,*
> *now at length the sword had pass'd.*

Jesus falls for the first time

The cobbled streets are uneven and the blood running down to his feet makes them slippery. It's hot, noisy, frightening. The cross weighs a ton and is widening the wounds of the flogging on his back. His mind drifts back to that terrible flogging. How did he survive it? The lead dumb-bells on the hissing leather thongs tearing his flesh open to the bone... how he had longed for the respite of unconsciousness!

Too late he realises he must not let his mind wander like that, he must concentrate on what he is doing, every step of it. Suddenly his toe catches a cobblestone; he trips and staggers. But his hands are gripping the cross and he can't reach out to save himself, so he crashes down.

> *He has given his angels charge over thee.*
> *In their hands they shall bear thee up*
> *Lest thou dash thy foot against a stone.*

So runs the psalm, and so it once was. But they won't, Lord, not anymore! That angelic guard was restrained and dismissed after they had thrown your assailants to the ground in the garden. You, dear Lord, had already burnt your boats when you handed over to Judas and the other apostles absolute power over your body at the Last Supper. Now, for good or ill, you are in our hands.

My dearest and most vulnerable Saviour, this fall of yours sounds all too familiar to me! Just like the way sin creeps up on me when I least expect it; and so there I go again, crashing down. Somehow I've *got* to get up, get going again. No sense in just lying there feeling sorry for myself. Lord, how weak I am; a burden not just to others but to myself. Not that I have any illusions about experiencing a road-to-Damascus type of transformation: I should be so lucky! No, odds on I'll repeat my mistakes many times before I die, but I've still got to keep on trying. Sure, one day God will transform me once and for all, but only when my most persistent efforts have been tried and found wanting.

And perhaps that's the hardest thing – having to learn from experience and then admit I'm not strong enough, that I can do absolutely nothing without your help, Lord. That's what I meant when I said a moment ago that my heaviest burden is myself: I am my own cross.

Jesus, do not let us take ourselves too seriously. Loving our neighbour is sometimes difficult, but never as difficult as loving and forgiving ourselves. Help us with your grace.

> *Oh, how sad and sore distress'd*
> *was that mother highly blest,*
> *of the sole-begotten One.*

Jesus meets his mother

This is how I imagine it. Jesus has just taken another of those terrible falls. The soldiers had lifted off the cross that was pinning him down and were yelling at him. He was at the end of his tether; everyone seemed against him.

Then, his face in the dust, he caught sight of a pair of feet he instantly recognized. He looked up and there she was. It was too late for her to hide the pain behind her eyes. But she knew what he needed now was strength, not sympathy. She squatted down beside him. 'Get up, son,' was all she would say, 'you know your Father's work must be done.' She didn't need to remind him of her love – he could never doubt that. She had always been a tower of strength when he was down and out and he had never needed that strength more than at this moment. What a mother! What a woman! He would have to remember to give her to us before he died, to be our mother too.

But first things first: for now, he had to get back on his feet. Never mind the crowd, the soldiers, the taunts, the pain. His mother's words were still ringing in his ears: '…your Father's work must be done.' She helped him up and he thanked her. She promised to stay close by him to the end, and they went on together. The commander of the Roman escort walked ahead of her to clear a path. Above the din he was thinking of his mother back home among the olive trees of their farm, and knew she'd want him to do that.

O Jesus, teach us to be gentle! We thank you for our mothers – their natural gentleness when we were tiny, helpless in their arms. Let that rub off on us and stick with us all our lives. Make us compassionate of other's sorrows, no matter what our duty requires of us.

In our lives we constantly have to find the right balance between duty and gentleness. The commander of the guard escorting your Son knew this. Committed to the sad duty of escorting a man to his death, yet in his humanity he found the grace to remember and practise the compassion learnt in his early years. Give us this special wisdom, Lord.

And now, Mother of our race, we turn to you. Keep us close beside you when the going gets tough; and when we fall and think we're down and out, remind us gently but firmly to get up and be about our Father's business.

Hail Mary, full of grace, the Lord is with thee. Blessed art thou among women and blessed is the fruit of thy womb, Jesus. Holy Mary, Mother of God, pray for us sinners now and at the hour of our death. Amen.

Christ above in torment hangs;
she beneath beholds the pangs
of her dying glorious Son.

Simon the Stranger carries the cross for him

One more heavy fall! If only he could reach the dreaded spot and get on with it. This numbing weakness was too much to bear; his legs kept buckling under the load. Almighty God though he was, he could take not another step without the help of sinful man. Two of the soldiers just kept goading, kicking, shouting...

Simon, a burly giant from North Africa, was in the crowd. What he saw sickened him, he had had enough. He roundly cursed the brutality of the soldiers. Viciously they turned on him: 'Right, Big-Mouth, you've just got yourself a job. You carry the bloody cross!' This caught him off guard. He was no common criminal; he had simply thought that anyone, no matter what he had done, should be shown a little decency – especially on the way to his death. He half turned, as if to make his escape into the crowd.

Then suddenly, their eyes met. He had heard about this man Jesus – who hadn't? – but had taken a lot of it with a pinch of salt. But those eyes! They seemed to look into the depths of his soul, as if his whole life were open to that penetrating gaze. And such silent pleading! Instantly his heart went out to this man. He instinctively knew he could have found himself in this very same position. After all, he was no saint; this could have been his cross.

He roughly pushed aside one of the soldiers who was kicking Jesus. The man turned on him, his hand on his short sword, but a growl from the corporal restrained him. Then, with his huge strength he helped Jesus gently to his feet. Their eyes met again though it could have been no more than a glance. Simon hardly noticed the soldiers laying the cross on his own shoulders as he gazed back at this extraordinary, wonderful man. He knew that from then on things would never be the same again. 'Come, my friend,' he heard himself say, 'we have work to do, you and I.'

✛ ✛ ✛ ✛ ✛ ✛ ✛

Lord, what a privilege it is to share your work and suffering! Simon shows us that most manly virtue of compassion tempering strength. Give us the grace never to stand fearfully by when we see another being bullied or abused; never to let pass unchallenged a cruel word or lie about another, whether to their face or behind their back. And when as a nation in a position of strength to intervene, never let us permit the subjugation of the weak by the mighty. Make us always ready and proud to help others with burdens too heavy to bear alone.

Jesus, touch our hearts as you did Simon's, that we may gladly give you a hand in any unsavoury task you set us.

> *Is there one who would not weep,*
> *whelm'd in miseries so deep,*
> *Christ's dear mother to behold?*

A Holy Woman Wipes the Face of Jesus (watercolour & gouache on paperboard), by James Tissot (1836–1906), Brooklyn Museum of Art

Here is another incident on his way to Calvary. We see Veronica, in defiance of the barbarous behaviour of Christ's tormentors, blocking his path to wipe his face before he continues on his way. Behind him in an archway on the right is a knot of four or five other women weeping to see him in this terrible state, with perhaps a couple of men. For the most part, others in the crowd appear more curious at the commotion than compassionate.

Veronica wipes his face with her shawl

'This damned sweat and blood, and the spittle trickling into my eyes and gumming them up. I can't see where I'm going. Even with Simon helping me, I'm terrified I might fall again,' he thought.

Suddenly, as if she had read his thoughts, a woman stepped out of the crowd and stopped him. One of the thorns was about to penetrate through his eyelid and blind him in that eye. Carefully she pulled it out and agonisingly shifted the cap of thorns slightly on his head. Then she took off her shawl and gently wiped his face with it. Her own eyes filled with tears until she could no longer see him properly, but now Jesus could see once more! He looked into the face of his benefactor and thought he recognized her. Hadn't he cured *her* blindness by making a paste of mud and spittle for her eyelids, and told her to wash it off? Yes, that was it! Now it was her turn to heal him. He smiled and thanked her.

Dear Lord, help me to remember how important small kindnesses are. Make me compassionate, not in fussy but in practical ways. Imprint your image on my mind and heart that I may never forget you. When others look on me may they see not me but you. Give me the compassion that will draw others to come to know you through what I do, and ultimately for what I shall become through your grace.

Jesus, we sinners are congenitally blind, determined to see others wrong so as to see ourselves right. Open our eyes, Saviour.

> *Can the human heart refrain*
> *from partaking in her pain,*
> *in that mother's pain untold?*

Jesus falls again

Just when he thought he was going to make it and the road seemed a little more even, the blood seemed to drain from his head for a moment. He staggered, lurched to one side and fell. Simon spotted what was about to happen just in time and with a mighty heave managed to throw the cross clear so that Jesus could reach out to break his fall. Even so, some of the thorns were driven deeper into his scalp.

When Simon threw the cross clear it hit one of the guard a glancing blow. The man cursed Simon furiously, then turned his wrath on Jesus. What a strange and uniquely human reaction is wrath! It has no place in God's nature, though many religious folk believe it to be for our own good that we hang onto the idea of God's wrath. Mankind is constantly projecting his own anger onto his distorted image of God, and religious wars have plagued him since the beginning. Jesus knew that his torment and crucifixion would one day convince the world of the pointlessness of wrath; that God's love for every individual is infinite and that our fears to the contrary are groundless. But first, he had to endure in silence, the Lamb being led to the slaughter. The dawn of understanding would be a long time a-coming – centuries perhaps, probably millennia – but come it would, the work of the Spirit whom he would send.

Help me, Lord, not to fear your imagined wrath. Instead, let me fear my failure to grow in the love you constantly extend to me. But if I must fear you, let it be the fear of hurting a Father who loves me without limit. Take away the rage of this world and the fear that's at the root of it. And start by calming the restless fears in our own hearts.

> *Bruised, derided, cursed, defiled,*
> *she beheld her tender child,*
> *all with bloody scourges rent.*

The weeping women

On one corner of the street was a knot of women, their shawls half hiding their faces, their eyes full of tears. They were weeping. Their pity moved him – he hadn't seen too much of it today – and for a moment his thoughts went back with sharp nostalgia to his childhood. He remembered that wonderful, redeeming human quality, mirrored throughout his animal creation: the gentleness of women. It reminded him how infinitely worthwhile the outcome of this dreadful day would be. Gradually, all mankind would learn to come to terms with the feminine side of its nature. That gentle suffusion of wisdom and acceptance would one day permeate the whole human race as evolution ran its inexorable course under the guidance of the feminine in its Creator-Lifegiver, the Holy Spirit. He recalled how much he loved this pilgrim race of his. But for the moment, cruelty had to run its course in order to burn itself out. He pressed on.

Jesus Christ, my Lord, my Saviour, my Judge and my God, give me the change of heart to weep for myself and for my children – indeed for the whole human race. Open our eyes to see what our sins have done to you, and what they continue to do to ourselves and to each other. Let my repentance show itself in action. Give me the will to deny myself, to fast regularly for the hundreds of millions of my brothers and sisters around the world who have not enough to live on, who live under oppression and injustice, and who do indeed weep for the children dying in their arms.

It's easy to get disheartened by the sea of misery around us, Jesus. But that won't do: tears are not enough. We can never know how much you can make of our tiny contributions. So, give us heart.

> *For the sins of his own nation,*
> *saw him hang in desolation,*
> *till his spirit forth he sent.*

The final fall

The sun beat down mercilessly. A small dog, alarmed and excited by the commotion, rushed across his path and he fell once more. This truly was very nearly the last straw. Even the soldiers noticed it and began to wonder whether he would have the strength to make it to Golgotha (an ugly word with an ugly meaning: the Place of the Skull.) More gently this time, they helped him up and allowed him a pause to catch his breath. Not for the first time he found himself wondering if he'd be able to get there. But then, in his divine power he saw those countless millions depending on him. He saw the millions; and he saw the individuals, each beyond price. He saw me. He saw my desperate need for him to get there if I were not to be lost for all eternity. 'No, not that…' he cried inwardly, and pressed on even before the corporal gave the order to continue.

Jesus, when I see this most terrible fall of all, let me remember the crime which grieves you above all others – the abuse and murder of children. We hear of countries where the sound of children's crying and incessant rocking on urine-soaked mattresses is blotted out behind unvisited orphanage walls so that the world can go about its business untroubled. We hear of small armies of innocent children kidnapped for indoctrination before being armed to murder. We know of children whose sacred little bodies – replicas of your own, Lord – are sold for profit or photographed for an unlimited market on a world-wide web of evil. And in our own land politicians continue to persuade themselves and their electorate that two hundred thousand unborn children a year can be disposed of, for a price. These are our sins, Lord, and we confess them. While such evil stalks the earth, never let us become complacent about our own complicity, inaction or silence.

Jesus, give us a burning thirst for justice in our land and throughout the world. Give us the courage to speak out when we can and should, and always to see you in the oppressed.

O thou mother! Fount of love!
Touch my spirit from above,
make my heart with thine accord.

Jesus is Stripped of His Garments, 1987 (oil on board), by Albert Herbert (b.1925), © England & Co. Gallery, London/By kind permission of the Estate of Albert Herbert/The Bridgeman Art Library

This horrific image of our cruelty and rage mocks us, not our victim. 'As the crowds were appalled on seeing him – so disfigured did he look that he seemed no longer human – so will the crowds be astonished at him, and kings stand speechless before him; for they shall see something never told and witness something never heard before.' *[Isaiah 52: 14-15].* Appalled we may well be, for his disfigurement was our work, not his. We nailed him to the Cross, crowned him with thorns, and tore the life out of him. Yet this was our madness that he came willingly to heal, and when we wake up and see what we have done our eyes will indeed be opened, our blindness lightened. Then we shall see something never told, never heard before.

Jesus is stripped

Almost unexpectedly, he was there. He'd made it up that endless hill! The appalling condition he was in heightened rather than dampened his relief. Now the only strength he'd need would be the power to stretch himself out on the terrible, wonderful, hideous cross. Simon took the full weight of it while Jesus moved clear and then the heavy timber fell from his shoulders too.

Simon turned back to this extraordinary man he had helped, this stranger he seemed to have known all his life as if in his dreams. On an impulse he embraced him. In that one human act he felt as if he had shed not only the burden of the cross but all the burdens he had ever carried, his anger and self-doubt, his sorrows, his pain. His throat tightened, his eyes stung. He knew he would meet this man again, though why or where he could not tell. 'God be with you, my friend,' he said, and fell back into the crowd.

The crowd watched and fell silent at this unanticipated moment of human dignity. It was as though it prepared them for the sudden shock as Jesus was stripped naked. He had been ready to make the ultimate fool of himself for love of me. His gaunt and terrible beauty held them and for the most part they remained hushed – though, then as now, yobs will always be with us.

Jesus, in stripping you naked the world takes its revenge, for it knows that you have stripped us in your mind of all the trappings with which we had hoped to hide this world's structures of power and order. You have seen through our lie, our Satan, and we don't like it. How dare you! we cry. *

But, Jesus, what would have been my reaction had I been there? Surely I would never have been able to forget what I saw and heard. But I was not around, there and then. I did not see or hear with my eyes and ears and memory. And yet, I have time after time after time been present at your Last Supper, your Crucifixion, your Resurrection. Indeed, I am privileged to be present at every event in your life, both on earth and in heaven, through the 'making present' of you in the Mass. Your Resurrection bridges the intervening miles and years. This I know; this I believe; and for this I thank you and worship you with all my soul's poor faculties of intellect, will and power to act. Even so, I am a weak and fickle child of your love. Without the stimuli of my senses I need your gift of faith to be constantly renewed in me. Grant this through your Spirit, my dearest naked Saviour.

Make me feel as thou hast felt;
make my soul to glow and melt
with the love of Christ my Lord.

* *I am indebted to Dom Sebastian Moore for this insight. He writes:*

'I saw Satan fall like lightning out of heaven.' What a vision! The huge lie woven into all cultures; the accepted contradictions so closely connected with exclusions of the unworthy; the absoluteness of power and consequent rivalry; the pretensions of empires; the lie that – in all these forms – is woven into the fabric of society, slips out, is gone: is gone, that is, in the mind of Jesus, for where else in any of the gospels does he say 'I saw'? There is a sudden stripping of the world, in his mind, of all its trappings. This vision weds him to the coming cross, his nakedness the world's vengeance for their being stripped in his eyes.

Sebastian Moore. 11 October 2005

Jesus is nailed to the cross

With measured experience they laid him on the cross and bound his hands and feet to it. The rest would be up to us. We'd have to do what we had to do – what our fear and pain, our blindness and our need to find someone to blame, someone to heal us, someone to… yes, kill – would make us do. Then everything would be all right. It would, wouldn't it? Oh please, God… Yes, everything would be all right. God would see to it. God would understand.

We started to drive the nails through wrists and heels into the hard wood. 'Father, forgive them. They don't know what they're doing,' he rasped. No pious utterance, this: simply the unvarnished truth. Indeed we did not – *do* not – know what we were and *are* doing! But one day, when his suffering and death have finally borne fruit as they must, then we shall understand. Then shall all the world finally be redeemed and ready to be handed back to the Father.

O Jesus, how we *long* for that day! How we long for an end to cruelty, a rooting-out from our hearts of the fear that drives us on to hurt and destroy. We know the days of this terrible human sickness are numbered, thanks to all you have endured. But your time-scale is cosmic, ours only human. I have barely a century on this earth (and most of the world far less than that) yet sometimes I dare hope to see fulfilment, a world at peace in my time. It's unreasonable, of course, but this longing matters because it drives me to work for your kingdom on earth. So, as we drive the nails through your hands and feet, remember it's our desperation at work as much as anything, Jesus. Indeed, we do *not* know what we are doing. Ask your Father to forgive us.

Our Father who art in heaven, hallowed be thy name. Thy kingdom come, thy will be done on earth as it is in heaven. Give us this day our daily bread, and forgive us our trespasses as we forgive those who trespass against us. And lead us – not into temptation, but deliver us from evil. Amen.

Holy Mother, pierce me through,
in my heart each wound renew
of my Saviour crucified.

*Plate 76 ex 'Jerusalem' (relief etching painted in orange with pen
& watercolour on paper), by William Blake (1757–1827),
Yale Center for British Art*

Rearing up from the dark earth, in the background we see the Tree of Life,
vast as a Giant Redwood. Hanging from it is its fruit, the Man who proclaimed
himself the Life, extending his arms in timeless surrender to God's will for his
beloved creation. Gazing up at him and mimicking him in loving worship
stands the lesser man for whom he died, the little Adam for whom the true
Adam gave his life that he might have life, his flesh that he might have
nourishment. The grace of God – his unchanging self-giving love – radiates
down upon the earth, and a glimmer of light in the background heralds the
dawn that will banish the purple shadows and darkness of death for good.

The death of Jesus

He feels the cross lurch and shudder as it is lifted high and planted in the revetted hole dug for it. Securing wedges are hammered in; the prophesied Tree of Life firmly planted. This Tree, foretold several thousand years before through pagan myths made Christian in the Eden prophecy, now bears its fruit; and we have been told that those who eat of the fruit will live forever. He is that fruit: we who eat of him shall find everlasting life.

His enemies jeer and crow, their revenge (so they believe) now assured. The soldiers divide his clothes among them, but throw dice for his seamless inner garment. Racked with cramps through loss of fluid from his appalling treatment, he gasps in thirst. They press a sponge of vinegar to his lips and he tastes it. It's bitter: he tastes our bitterness.

At the foot of the cross he sees his mother with St John and Mary Magdalene our representatives, standing by him when so many other of his friends have slunk away. He remembers his plan to give her to us and us to her: she is indeed the true Mother of our race, our Eve.

Finding the will even in this terrible agony to pray, he cries out to his Father in the words of the psalm, 'My God, my *God*, why have you forsaken me?' For these are *our* words and always have been throughout history, words cried out in perplexity and loneliness by the millions, words now cried out by God to God. What greater proof can we ask that he is truly Emanuel, God-with-us, in death as in life?

In his struggle for life, so much a part of our human nature and therefore even more a part of this most human of all men, he must at last succumb. His strength fails, he has given everything and his work is over. 'Father, into your hands I commend my spirit.' And it is done.

Nothing ever again need come between God and Man; the temple veil is rent from top to bottom by triumphant angels. Man is once and forever at one with God: atonement is achieved. Amen.

✛ ✛ ✛ ✛ ✛ ✛ ✛

Loving Saviour, look where your reckless love for mankind has brought you! Had you really bargained for all this? Death you had always accepted, as part of being human, of being Emanuel. But, the death of a disgraced criminal on a cross? And yet, being *the* Scapegoat to end all scapegoating had to be something we could never forget, something to stand the test of time. And it has, it will.

This I ask you, Lover of my soul: be there at my death. Take my hand, lead me through. And when I jump, catch me. Amen.

Jesus, because you truly died for us we call your death the sacrifice of the cross. But let not fine words disguise what it truly was: your murder at our hands. We are filled with gratitude and shame.

> *Let me share with thee his pain,*
> *who for all my sins was slain,*
> *who for me in torments died.*

The Lament of Christ (panel), by Peter Rubens (1577–1640),
Kunsthistoriches Museum, Vienna

The inert body of Jesus is taken down from the Cross and placed on the ground at the mouth of the tomb in which he will be laid when the men have completed the preparations inside. His mother has already held him in her arms at the foot of the Cross, and kneels weeping at the right of the picture. Now he is supported by Mary Magdalene, Mary the mother of James, and Salome. On the left, a bowl of water has been used to wash away some of the evidence of the appalling treatment he suffered. Soon the men will lift him onto the shelf and wind him in the grave cloth.

Jesus is returned to his mother

What a day it had been! The final three hours on the cross had seemed an eternity. And all those extraordinary events, as if the foundations of the world were moving. First the blotting-out of the sun (was it an eclipse?) accompanied by the sudden cold and the silence of birds and animals. Even the priests and leaders piped down. Then, to top it all, an earthquake, the earth itself trembling at the coming death of its King. The Centurion seemed to recognize it: 'Indeed this man *was* a Son of God,' he had said. The crowd, now silent, appeared uneasy at what they had done and hurried back into the city walls as if seeking protection from an unseen force. To speed them on their way came a sudden squall of torrential rain. The water washed the blood from his body, carrying it in rivulets into an earth thirsty for communion with its Maker.

A knot of his closest friends remained around his mother in the soaking, cleansing torrent. With a ladder, some nail-pullers and ropes they worked silent and numb until he was free from the cross; then laid him in the arms of his mother and left her alone for a while. She squatted on her haunches in the mud, cradling his head in her knees. What was it Simeon had said when she and Joseph had brought their baby to the temple thirty-three years ago? Something about a sword piercing her heart... Now at last she could let go her pain and hold on to her son – a peace of a sort, not unlike the peace of holding him after the anguish of giving birth. Then, she had half sensed the many partings; but now, no-one could ever take him from her again. Now her strength would no longer be needed. Now at last her heart could break and the hot tears could run and run.

✛ ✛ ✛ ✛ ✛ ✛ ✛

Dear Mother, now that he has gone we turn again to you. Through his gift you are the flawless vessel of his grace, his one perfect companion in all his suffering, in life and in death. Though there were times when you didn't understand, you never doubted him. Even now, when everything seems to have come to a disastrous and appalling dead end, deep down your trust doesn't falter. This puts you in the strongest possible position to plead to him for us, your children – which is why he gave you to us. Dear Mother, we expect nothing less.

Hail, Holy Queen, Mother of Mercy. Hail our life, our sweetness and our hope. To thee do we cry, poor banished children of Eve. To thee do we send up our sighs, mourning and weeping in this vale of tears. Turn then, most gracious advocate, thine eyes of mercy towards us, and after this our exile show unto us the blessed fruit of thy womb, Jesus. O clement, O loving, O sweet virgin Mary!

Let me mingle tears with thee,
mourning him who mourn'd for me,
all the days that I may live.

✝ THE FOURTEENTH STATION ✝

Jesus is laid in the tomb

Evening was approaching, it was the Preparation Day and they had to hurry to lay the body to rest before the Sabbath. There wouldn't be time to finish the job, but at least he would be under cover. Joseph of Arimathaea, a secret follower of Jesus, had a tomb nearby, newly hewn from the rock for himself. He led them to it. There was a stone shelf down one side. They placed the body on the five-yard linen shroud, arranged his arms across his front and placed a cloth over his face. Then they folded the linen back to cover him completely, binding it in place with long winding cloths... like the swaddling bands when he came into the world in that other cave not many miles away. No time to arrange the full hundredweight of spikenard, myrrh and aloes: they would return the day after tomorrow and do a proper job. They had hardly exchanged a word during the last hour, and then only in murmurs. It seemed right. They stood for a moment and looked down on him. They had had such high hopes; and now this. Moving outside, they rolled back the stone to keep out animals, and went to find his mother at John's place. It had been a long, long day.

As they left, they met a small guard sent by the chief priests, coming to seal the tomb and keep watch for grave robbers. What a ludicrous idea! Still, they had no objection. In fact it would be quite reassuring to know he'd still be there safe and sound when they came back after the Sabbath, the day when God and man took their rest.

Little did they know!

Glory be to the Father, and to the Son, and to the Holy Spirit – as it was in the beginning, is now, and ever shall be, world without end. Amen.

By the cross with thee to stay,
there with thee to weep and pray,
is all I ask of thee to give.

The Dead Christ (tempera on panel), by Hans Holbein the Younger
(1479–1543), Kunstmuseum, Basel

His gaunt and ravaged body can at last rest on the cold shelf. His hand, pierced and greyed with bruising, now lies limp after supporting its load for three long hours. One finger won't curl up – evidence of a tendon severed by the nail. His jaw will be bound closed and a cloth placed over his face. Then, with a small quantity of herbs and spices until the full load is brought after the Sabbath, he will be swaddled in the binding cloth and the tomb made secure until they return. There is nothing more they can do. Nothing more anyone can do. Only his mother refuses to give up hope. Deep down, beneath her tears, she knows there has to be another chapter. But there's no point in telling the others… though she did half say something to John, and he seemed to understand. 'God knows what he is doing', he had said.

THE END AND THE BEGINNING

APPENDIX

National Variations in the Meditations on the Stations of the Cross

A comparison of the fourteen Stations of the Cross used in this country and much of Europe and America with those used by Spanish and Catalan-speaking peoples is interesting. Stations held in common are highlighted in grey and it will be seen that half are not. Apart from the fourth sorrowful mystery, the Way of the Cross (which by implication includes in the Rosary most of these Stations' events), other Stations also meditated upon in those **sorrowful mysteries** are marked with a star (*). So there is quite a degree of overlap.

STATION	CHURCHES IN BRITAIN	CHURCHES IN SPAIN AND CATALONIA
1	Jesus is condemned by Pilate	Jesus in agony in the Garden *
2	Jesus accepts his Cross	Jesus is betrayed by Judas
3	Jesus falls for the first time	Jesus before Caiaphas
4	Jesus meets his mother	Jesus is denied by Peter
5	Jesus is helped by Simon	Jesus is condemned by Pilate
6	Jesus meets Veronica who wipes his face	Jesus is crowned with thorns *
7	Jesus falls a second time	Jesus accepts his Cross
8	Jesus meets the weeping women	Jesus meets the weeping women
9	Jesus falls for the third time	Jesus is helped by Simon
10	Jesus is stripped naked	Jesus is nailed to the Cross
11	Jesus is nailed to the Cross	Jesus comforts the Good Thief
12	Jesus dies on the Cross *	Jesus gives his mother to us
13	Jesus is taken down from the Cross	Jesus dies on the Cross *
14	Jesus is laid in the tomb	Jesus is laid in the tomb

In addition to the fourteen Stations customarily used in Britain and much of the Catholic world in the West, Poland includes four more, shown below. Note that two of these marked with a tick are also topics to be found in the **glorious mysteries** of the Rosary. The 15th Station listed below is often also included in Britain.

STATION	CHURCHES IN POLAND	
15	Jesus rises from the dead	✓
16	Jesus shows Thomas his wounds	
17	Jesus commands Peter to feed his sheep	
18	Jesus ascends to his Father	✓